Atoms and Molecules Experiments
Using Ice, Salt, Marbles, and More

One Hour or Less Science Experiments

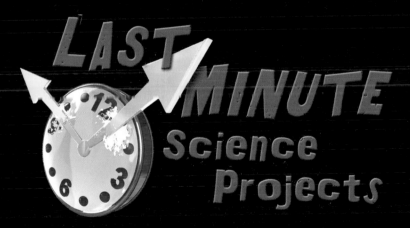

LAST MINUTE Science Projects

ROBERT GARDNER

Enslow Publishers, Inc.
40 Industrial Road
Box 398
Berkeley Heights, NJ 07922
USA

http://www.enslow.com

Library of Congress Cataloging-in-Publication Data

Gardner, Robert, 1929–
    Atoms and molecules experiments using ice, salt, marbles, and more : one hour
or less science experiments / Robert Gardner.
        p. cm. — (Last-minute science projects)
    Includes index.
    ISBN 978-0-7660-3961-2
    1. Matter—Constitution—Experiments—Juvenile literature. 2. Atoms—Experiments—
Juvenile literature. 3. Molecules—Experiments—Juvenile literature. I. Title.
    QC173.16.G368 2012
    507.8—dc23
                        2011026508

Future editions:
Paperback ISBN 978-1-4644-0144-2
ePUB ISBN 978-1-4645-1051-9
PDF ISBN 978-1-4646-1051-6

Printed in the United States of America

032012 Lake Book Manufacturing, Inc., Melrose Park, IL

10 9 8 7 6 5 4 3 2 1

Illustration Credits: © 2011 by Stephen Rountree (www.stephenrountree.com), pp. 9, 13, 15, 17, 19, 23,
25, 27, 29, 33, 35, 37, 43; Jonathan Moreno, pp. 11, 21 (b); Tom LaBaff and Stephanie LaBaff, pp. 21 (a),
31, 39, 41.

Cover Photos: Shutterstock.com

Contents

🎀 Contains ideas for more science fair projects.

Are You Running Late?

Is your science project due tomorrow? Have you put it off until now? Here is a solution! You can do the experiments in this book in one hour or less. In fact, some of them can be done in 30 minutes, 15 minutes, or as little as 5 minutes. Even if you have plenty of time for your next science project or are just looking for some fun experiments, you can enjoy this book, too.

Most of the experiments are followed by a "Keep Exploring" section. There you will find ideas for projects or experiments in which the details are left to you. You can design your own experiments, **under adult supervision,** when you have more time. Sometimes you may need a partner. Work with someone who likes to experiment as much as you do! Please follow any safety warnings and work with **an adult** when it is suggested.

This is a book about atoms and molecules—the tiny particles that make up matter. An atom is the smallest particle of a chemical element, which cannot be split into simpler substances. All the atoms in an element have the same number of protons and electrons. A molecule is the smallest particle of a chemical element or compound that has the properties of the element or compound. The molecules that make up compounds such as water or sugar contain atoms of different elements. Water molecules, for example, have two hydrogen atoms and one oxygen atom. To show the makeup of a molecule, we can write a chemical formula. For a water molecule, we write the formula H_2O, which shows that water molecules have two hydrogen atoms (H_2) and one oxygen atom (O).

The Scientific Method

Different sciences use different ways of experimenting. Depending on the problem, one method is likely to be better than another. Designing a new medicine for heart disease and finding evidence of water on Mars require different experiments.

Even with these differences, most scientists use the scientific method. This includes: making an observation, coming up with a question, making a hypothesis (a possible answer to the question) and a prediction (an if-then statement), designing and conducting an experiment, analyzing results, drawing conclusions, and deciding if the hypothesis is true or false. Scientists share their results. They publish articles in science journals.

Once you have a question, you can make a hypothesis. Your hypothesis is a possible answer to the question (what you think will happen). For example, you might hypothesize that molecules of water will be attracted by electrical charges. Then you test your hypothesis.

In most cases you should do a controlled experiment. This means having two groups that are treated the same except for the thing being tested. That thing is called a variable. For example, to test the hypothesis above, you might have two identical thin streams of water from two faucets. You would hold a charged object near one stream and an identical but uncharged object near the other. If water is attracted to the charged object and not to the uncharged object, you would conclude that your hypothesis is true.

The results of one experiment often lead to another question. Or they may send you off in another direction. Whatever the results, something can be learned from every experiment!

Science Fairs

All of the investigations in this book contain ideas that might lead you to a science fair project. However, judges at science fairs do not reward projects or experiments that are simply copied from a book. For example, a diagram of an atom would not impress most judges; however, an experiment that provides an estimate of the size of a molecule would gain their attention.

Science fair judges tend to reward creative thought and imagination. It is difficult to be creative or imaginative unless you are really interested in your project. Therefore, try to choose an investigation that excites you. And before you jump into a project, consider, too, your own talents and the cost of the materials you will need.

If you decide to use an experiment or idea found in this book for a science fair, find ways to modify or extend it. This should not be difficult. As you do investigations, you will get new ideas. You will think of questions that experiments can answer. The experiments will make great science fair projects because the ideas are your own and are interesting to you.

Your Notebook

Your notebook, as any scientist will tell you, is a valuable possession. It should contain ideas you may have as you experiment, sketches you may draw, calculations you make, and hypotheses you may suggest. It should include a description of every experiment you do, the data you record, such as voltages, currents, resistors, weights, and so on. It should also contain the results of your experiments, graphs you draw, and any conclusions you may be able to reach based on your results.

Safety First

1. Do any experiments or projects from this book or of your own design under the adult supervision of a science teacher or other knowledgeable adult.

2. Read all instructions carefully before proceeding with a project. If you have questions, check with your supervisor before going any further.

3. Always wear safety goggles when doing experiments that could cause particles to enter your eyes. Tie back long hair. Do not wear sandals.

4. Do not eat or drink while experimenting. Never taste substances being used (unless instructed to do so).

5. Do not touch chemicals, and do not let water drops fall on a hot lightbulb.

6. The liquid in some thermometers is mercury (a dense liquid metal). It is dangerous to touch mercury or breathe mercury vapor. When doing these experiments, use only non-mercury thermometers, such as those filled with alcohol. If you have a mercury thermometer in the house, ask an adult if it can be taken to a local thermometer exchange location.

7. Do only those experiments that are described in the book or those that have been approved by an adult.

8. Maintain a serious attitude while conducting experiments. Never engage in horseplay or play practical jokes.

9. At the end of every activity, clean all materials used and put them away. Then wash your hands thoroughly with soap and water.

One Hour or Less

Here are experiments with atoms and molecules that you can do in one hour or less. You don't have any time to lose, so let's get started!

1 How Big Is a Molecule?

What's the Plan?

Let's estimate the size of a molecule.

What You Do

1. Add 1 cm of water to a clean shallow tray.

2. When the water is still, sprinkle a small amount of talcum powder or chalk dust on it.

3. Bend a fine piece of wire into a narrow V-shape. Wind the ends of the wire together. Clamp them with a clothespin (Figure 1a). Dip the V-shaped part of the wire into some alcohol to clean it.

4. When the wire dries, dip the tip of the V into oleic acid (a liquid). A tiny drop will cling to the wire.

5. Have a partner hold the clothespin. Using a magnifier and a ruler, estimate the diameter (d) of the drop (Figure 1b).

6. Assume the drop is a cube. To estimate the drop's volume, cube its diameter (d x d x d).

WHAT YOU NEED:

- water
- cafeteria tray or other shallow plastic tray
- talcum powder or chalk dust
- fine piece of wire about 6 in long
- clothespin
- rubbing alcohol
- oleic acid (borrow from a science lab)
- a partner
- magnifier
- metric ruler
- calculator (optional)

7. Dip the tip of the wire several times into the center of the water in the tray. The oleic acid will spread into a thin layer, pushing the powder outward and making a clear circle. Assume the circular layer is one molecule thick.

8. Measure the average diameter of the oleic acid circle (Figure 1c). Then calculate the area covered by the oleic acid.

9. Calculate the thickness of the oleic acid circle, which is the thickness of an oleic acid molecule.

What's Going On?

The author estimated the diameter of the drop to be 0.5 mm, so its volume was $(0.5 \text{ mm})^3$ and 0.5 mm x 0.5 mm x 0.5 mm = 0.125 mm^3. The circle's diameter was 200 mm; its area (πr^2) was $\pi(100 \text{ mm})^2$ or $31,400 \text{ mm}^2$. The thickness of the oleic acid circle or of one molecule was its volume divided by its area, which was 4 millionths of a millimeter.

$$\frac{0.125 \text{ mm}^3}{31,400 \text{ mm}^2} = 0.000004 \text{ mm}$$

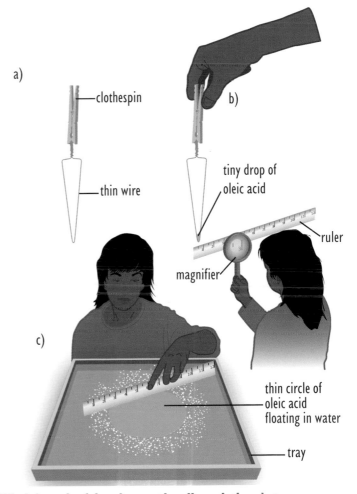

a)

clothespin

b)

thin wire

tiny drop of oleic acid

ruler

magnifier

c)

thin circle of oleic acid floating in water

tray

Figure 1. a) Bend a fine piece of wire into a V-shape. Wind the ends of the wire together. Use a clothespin to hold the wire. b) Use a magnifier and a ruler to estimate the diameter (d) of the drop. c) Measure the average diameter of the oleic acid layer that floats on the water.

2 Gases, Temperature, and Molecules

What's the Plan?

Let's see how the volume of a gas is affected by temperature.

What You Do

1. Push a small lump of clay into one end of a clear plastic soda straw. Add a little more clay to be sure the end of the straw is sealed.

2. Using small pieces of clear tape, attach the straw to a metric ruler. Line up the 0-cm line of the ruler with the level that the clay is pushed into the straw's end (Figure 2a).

3. Put a drop of blue food coloring in a cup. Add a tablespoon of water. Fill an eyedropper with the colored water.

4. Fill a tall glass, jar, or vase with very hot water. Then insert the straw and ruler until the straw's top is about 1 cm above the hot water in the glass. Do not let hot water enter the straw.

5. Using the eyedropper, carefully insert two drops of colored water into the top of the straw. You have made a water "plug" that traps the warm air inside (Figure 2b).

WHAT YOU NEED:

- clay
- clear plastic soda straw
- clear tape
- metric ruler
- eyedropper
- cup
- water
- blue food coloring
- tablespoon
- tall glass, jar, or vase
- very hot tap water
- room temperature water
- ice water

6. Put your straw and ruler into a glass of water at room temperature. The volume of air in the straw will shrink and the water plug will fall lower as the air contracts.

7. Put the apparatus into ice water. The gas in the straw will shrink some more.

What's Going On?

At temperatures above absolute zero (–273°C), all molecules are moving. The higher the temperature, the faster the molecules move. When the molecules of a gas move faster, they take up more space, so the volume of a gas increases as the temperature increases.

Keep Exploring—If You Have More Time!

- Do experiments to show that you have made a gas thermometer that can measure temperatures.

- Use your gas thermometer and a regular thermometer to predict the temperature of absolute zero.

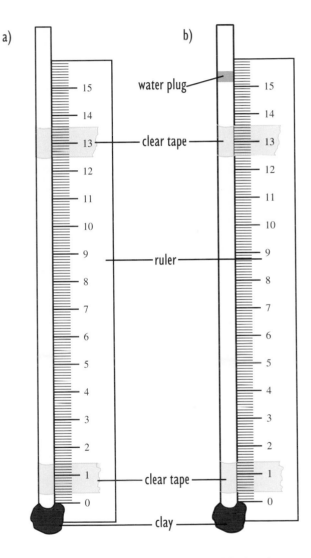

Figure 2. a) A clear plastic straw, its end filled with clay, is taped to a metric ruler. b) A water plug is added to the open end of the straw in order to trap a volume of air in the straw.

3 "Salt Crystals" Greatly Enlarged

What's the Plan?

Let's see what salt (sodium chloride) looks like at the atomic level.

WHAT YOU NEED:

- 14 styrofoam spheres two inches in diameter
- 14 styrofoam spheres one inch in diameter
- toothpicks

What You Do

1. Use 14 styrofoam spheres two inches in diameter to build the three structures shown in Figure 3a. Each sphere represents a chloride ion (Cl^-). Use toothpicks to hold them together.

2. Place the 4-sphere structure on top of a 5-sphere structure. Then put another 5-sphere structure on top of the 4-sphere structure (Figure 3b). You have built the basic form of a cubic close packing crystal, such as salt.

3. Place 14 styrofoam spheres one inch in diameter in the openings between the chloride ions. These spheres represent sodium ions (Na^+). You have built the basic structure of a sodium chloride crystal (Figure 3c).

What's Going On?

Sodium ions have a diameter of 0.19 nanometers (a nanometer is one billionth of a meter). Chloride ions have a diameter of 0.362 nanometers. The ratio of their diameters (1.9) is very close to 2, which is why we used 1-inch and 2-inch spheres.

As you can see, each chloride ion is surrounded by six sodium ions and each sodium ion is surrounded by six chloride ions. The positive and negative charges balance and are evenly spread throughout the crystal.

Keep Exploring—If You Have More Time!

- Crystals form in different ways. You might investigate and build models of other ways that atoms or ions pack together in crystals such as hexagonal close packing and body-centered cubic packing.

- How do scientists determine the structure of crystals?

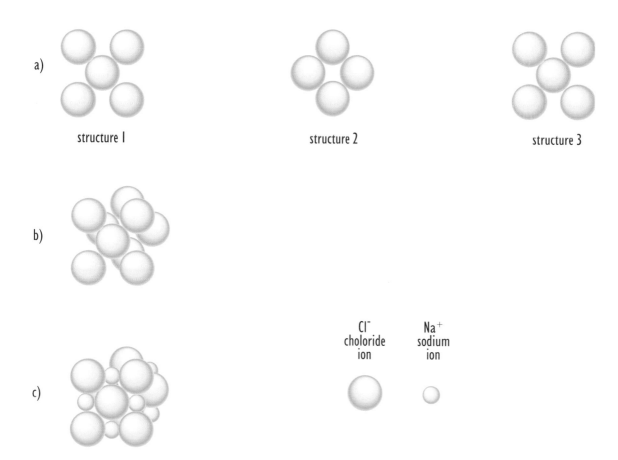

a)

structure 1   structure 2   structure 3

b)

c)

Cl⁻
choloride
ion

Na⁺
sodium
ion

Figure 3. a) Using two-inch spheres, build the layers you will use to make a model of a cubic close packing crystal. b) Put structure 2 on structure 1. Then put structure 3 on structure 2. c) Place the one-inch spheres in the spaces between the two-inch spheres.

13

4 When Molecules Exchange Atoms

What's the Plan?

Let's see what happens in a chemical reaction.

What You Do

1. Pour 50 mL (1/4 cup) of white vinegar—acetic acid ($C_2H_4O_2$)—into a flask or small bottle.

2. Place the end of a funnel in the mouth of a balloon (Figure 4a). Pour one teaspoon of baking soda (sodium bicarbonate) into the balloon. Tap the funnel to get all the baking soda ($NaHCO_3$) into the balloon.

3. Pull the neck of the balloon over the top of the vessel containing the vinegar. Then lift the balloon (Figure 4b) to pour the baking soda into the vinegar. Watch the chemical reaction occur and the balloon inflate until the bubbling stops.

4. Place a small lump of clay on the bottom of a wide jar. Use the clay to support an upright birthday candle (Figure 4c). Ask an adult to light the candle.

5. Let the candle burn until the candle flame is well below the top of the jar.

6. Squeeze or twist the neck of the balloon so the gas cannot escape. Then remove the balloon from the flask or bottle. Put the neck of the balloon into the jar with the burning candle. Slowly release the gas (Figure 4d). The candle flame will be extinguished.

> **WHAT YOU NEED:**
> - medicine cup or metric measuring cup
> - white vinegar
> - flask or small bottle
> - funnel
> - balloon
> - teaspoon
> - baking soda
> - clay
> - wide jar
> - birthday candle
> - an adult
> - matches

What's Going On?

The chemical equation below shows what happened. The atoms in the sodium bicarbonate and acetic acid molecules rearranged to form sodium acetate, water, and carbon dioxide gas, which filled the balloon and then, like a CO_2 fire extinguisher, put out the flame by displacing the oxygen.

$$NaHCO_3 + C_2H_4O_2 \rightarrow NaC_2H_3O_2 + H_2O + CO_2$$

sodium bicarbonate	acetic acid	sodium acetate	water	carbon dioxide

Keep Exploring—If You Have More Time!

Will other acids react with baking soda to produce carbon dioxide? Try lemon juice, grapefruit juice, and solutions of citric acid (Tang™ and Kool-Aid™).

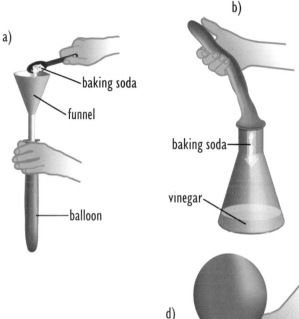

a)

baking soda

funnel

balloon

b)

baking soda

vinegar

d)

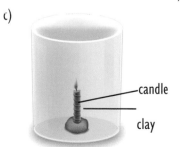

c)

candle

clay

Figure 4. a) Add a teaspoon of baking soda to a balloon. b) Pull the neck of the balloon over the mouth of the vessel that contains the vinegar. Add the baking soda to the vinegar. c) Light a birthday candle in a wide jar. d) Slowly release the balloonful of gas into the jar that holds the burning candle.

30 Minutes or Less

Pressed for time? Here are some experiments you can do in 30 minutes, more or less.

5 Atoms and Molecules: Sink or Float?

What's the Plan?

Let's see if knowing the masses of atoms and molecules will allow us to predict whether one gas will sink or float when mixed with another. From the periodic table, we found the masses of several atoms in atomic mass units (Table 1). One AMU is approximately the mass of one hydrogen atom.

Table 1: The atomic masses of four common elements.		
Element	Element Symbol	Atomic mass (AMU)
hydrogen	H	1
carbon	C	12
nitrogen	N	14
oxygen	O	16

What You Do

1. Pour about 2 cm (1 in) of water into a 4-liter (1-gal) plastic pail. Add a dozen seltzer tablets to the water. The fizzing reaction of the seltzer and water produces carbon dioxide gas (CO_2).

2. Using some bubble-making solution and a wand, quickly make some air-filled bubbles (Figure 5a). Let the bubbles fall into the pail. You may have to move the pail so it lies under the falling bubbles. Watch the air bubbles float on the carbon dioxide (Figure 5b).

What's Going On?

Carbon dioxide molecules have a molecular mass of 44 AMUs because $12 + (2 \times 16) = 44$. Air is about 2/10 oxygen (O_2) and 8/10 nitrogen (N_2). The average molecular mass of air is about 28.8 because:

$$0.2 \times 32 + 0.8 \times 28 = 28.8.$$

As you've seen, air-filled bubbles float on carbon dioxide. So knowing the molecular masses of these two gases does allow us to predict that air will float on carbon dioxide, at least until they diffuse into one another.

Keep Exploring—If You Have More Time!

- Molecules of cooking oil weigh hundreds of AMUs. Water molecules (H_2O) have a mass of 18 AMUs ($[2 \times 1] + 16$). Will water float on cooking oil? Try it! Explain your result.

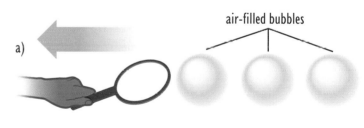

air-filled bubbles

air-filled bubble floating on CO_2

Figure 5. a) Make some air-filled bubbles. b) Watch the air-filled bubbles float on the carbon dioxide.

6 Where Does the Salt Go?

What's the Plan?

Let's see what happens to the total volume when we dissolve salt in water.

What You Do

1. Add 20 mL of salt to a clean, dry graduated cylinder. Pour the salt into a beaker or glass.

2. Use the graduated cylinder to measure 90 mL of water. Add the water to the salt.

3. Stir the mixture until all the salt dissolves (disappears in the water).

4. Pour the salt water into the graduated cylinder. Record its volume.

5. To see why the volume is much less than 110 mL, pour marbles into a dry graduated cylinder. Then add fine, dry sand (Figure 6a). Watch the sand move between the marbles.

What's Going On?

You probably found that the volume of the salt solution was considerably less than 110 mL, which was the volume of salt (20 mL) plus water (90 mL). The reason is that salt particles (ions) can fit between water molecules just as sand

particles can fit between marbles. Also, the volume of salt included some air between the salt particles. The air did not dissolve in the water.

Keep Exploring—If You Have More Time!

- Try sugar instead of salt. Are the results the same?

- Set up the experiment shown in Figure 6b. The test tube on the right contains only water. The test tube on the left contains water and two lumps of rock salt. What happens to the volume as the rock salt dissolves? Can you explain why it happens?

- As you have seen, volume 1 (salt) + volume 2 (water) may not equal their sum when they are mixed. Design and do experiments to see if mass 1 + mass 2 always equals the sum of their masses when the two are mixed.

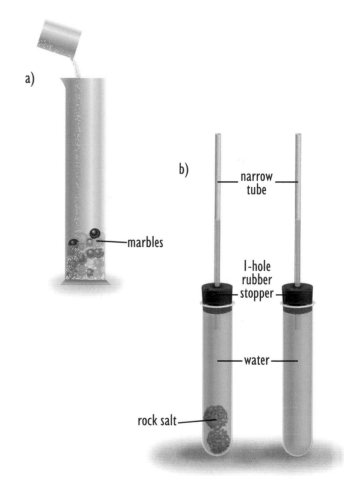

Figure 6. a) Add dry sand to marbles. Notice how the sand particles fit between the marbles.
b) What happens to the volume as the salt dissolves?

7 Do Some "Molecules" Conduct Electricity?

WHAT YOU NEED:
- teaspoon
- water
- graduated cylinder
- table salt
- water vial or medicine cups
- toothpick
- 2 paper clips
- 3 wires with alligator clips
- 6-volt battery
- flashlight bulb
- bulb holder
- sugar

What's the Plan?

Let's see if some molecules will conduct electricity. We'll dissolve them in water so they are free to move.

What You Do

1. Add a teaspoonful of salt to 25 mL of water in a vial or medicine cup. Stir to dissolve some of the salt.

2. Slide two paper clips onto the side of the vial or cup as shown in Figure 7a. Use wires with alligator clips to connect the paper clips to a 6-volt lantern battery and a flashlight bulb in a bulb holder as shown in the drawing.

3. If the bulb lights, you know that a salt solution conducts electricity.

4. Repeat the experiment using sugar instead of salt.

What's Going On?

Salt is a compound that consists of positive and negative ions (Figure 7b). Ions are charged atoms that have lost or gained one or more electrons. Ordinary table salt, sodium chloride (NaCl), consists of equal numbers of positive sodium ions (Na^+) and negative chloride ions (Cl^-). As you saw, these ions allow a solution of salt to conduct electricity. Sugar molecules ($C_{12}H_{22}O_{11}$) do not form ions in water. Consequently, a sugar solution will not conduct electricity.

Keep Exploring—If You Have More Time!

- Try doing Experiment 7 with Epsom salt. What do you find? What does it tell you about Epsom salt?

- Try doing Experiment 7 with cooking oil. What do you find? What does it tell you about cooking oil?

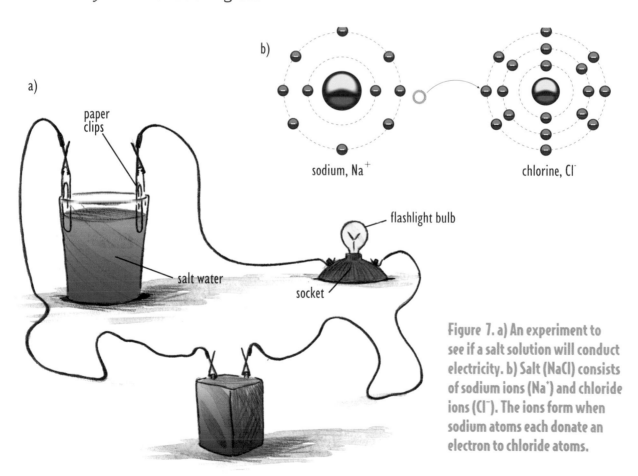

b)

sodium, Na$^+$

chlorine, Cl$^-$

paper clips

salt water

flashlight bulb

socket

a)

Figure 7. a) An experiment to see if a salt solution will conduct electricity. b) Salt (NaCl) consists of sodium ions (Na$^+$) and chloride ions (Cl$^-$). The ions form when sodium atoms each donate an electron to chloride atoms.

21

8 Can We Separate Atoms From Molecules?

WHAT YOU NEED:

- scissors
- aluminum foil
- ruler
- small frying pan
- stove
- measuring spoons
- sugar
- an adult
- safety glasses
- forceps
- oven mitt

What's the Plan?

Let's see if we can separate atoms of one element from the atoms of hydrogen, oxygen, and carbon that are joined in molecules of sugar, which has the chemical formula $C_{12}H_{22}O_{11}$.

What You Do

1. Use scissors to cut a square piece of aluminum foil about 8 cm (3 in) on a side.

2. Put the foil in a small frying pan on a stove (Figure 8a).

3. Place 1/4 teaspoon of sugar on the aluminum foil.

4. Under adult supervision and wearing safety glasses, carefully heat the pan that holds the sugar. You will see the sugar turn a brownish color as it melts.

5. Keep heating. The sugar darkens, bubbles, and emits a vapor. Continue heating until it stops bubbling. By now it should be completely black.

6. Wait about ten minutes for the mixture and pan to cool. Put on an oven mitt. Then use forceps to remove the aluminum foil that holds the black carbon (Figure 8b).

7. Carefully break the carbon apart. You will see it is filled with holes formed by bubbles of gaseous water.

What's Going On?

At high temperatures the sugar molecules melt and then decompose into carbon (C) atoms, the black substance that was left, and water vapor (H_2O) that escaped as a gas.

Keep Exploring—If You Have More Time!

- Under adult supervision, design and do an experiment to show that the vapor that escapes during the heating is really water.

a) sugar   aluminum foil

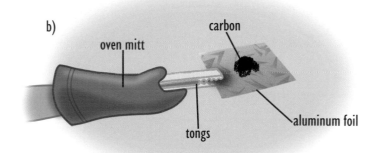
b) oven mitt   carbon   tongs   aluminum foil

Figure 8. a) Put some sugar on a piece of aluminum foil in a frying pan.
b) Use forceps to remove the aluminum foil and black carbon.

23

9 When Molecules Collide

What's the Plan?

Let's show what happens when molecules collide. Usually these collisions are elastic. This means no kinetic (motion) energy is lost.

What You Do

1. To see a nearly elastic collision, drop a Super Ball® onto a smooth floor. The ball will rise to nearly the height from which it fell (Figure 9a).

2. Mold clay into a ball. Drop the ball onto the floor. It simply flattens. It doesn't bounce at all (Figure 9b). This is an inelastic collision. All the kinetic energy is changed to thermal energy (heat).

3. Drop a tennis or a golf ball onto the floor. It will bounce, but not as high as the Super Ball®. Like many collisions, this one is partially elastic. Some kinetic energy is lost.

4. To make a model of a molecular collision, place a marble near the center of a level grooved ruler. Roll a smaller marble into the one at rest (Figure 9c). Then roll a larger marble into it.

5. Place a small lump of soft clay on a marble at rest. Roll another marble into the clay side of the marble and observe what happens (Figure 9d).

What's Going On

Most molecular collisions are like the ones in step 4; however, they are completely elastic. A collision between different molecules, as illustrated in step 5, can result in a chemical change as a new molecule forms. For example, some collisions between carbon (C) and oxygen (O_2) molecules produce molecules of carbon dioxide (CO_2).

Keep Exploring—If You Have More Time!

- Investigate collisions between billiard balls, marbles, baseballs, and other spheres. Are any of the collisions nearly elastic?

- For chemical reactions to occur, molecules must collide. How do you think temperature will affect the rate of a reaction? Do an experiment to test your hypothesis.

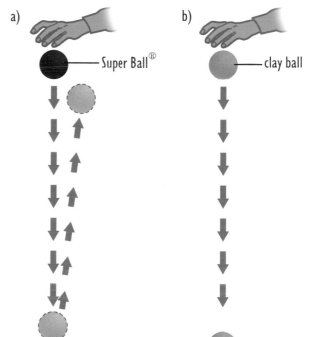

a) Super Ball®

b) clay ball

Figure 9.
a) A nearly elastic collision
b) An inelastic collision
c) A "molecular" collision
d) A "molecular" collision resulting in a chemical change (a new molecule is formed)

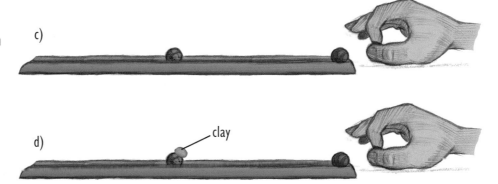

c)

d) clay

15 Minutes or Less

Time is really in short supply if you need an experiment you can do in 15 minutes. Here to rescue you are more experiments you can do quickly.

10 Modeling a Chemical Reaction

What's the Plan?

Let's make a model to show how hydrogen and oxygen combine to form water.

WHAT YOU NEED:

• clothespins

• paper clips

What You Do

1. Gather some clothespins and paper clips. Clothespins will represent oxygen atoms; paper clips will represent the smaller hydrogen atoms.

2. Join the clothespins in pairs (Figure 10a). Do the same with the paper clips. Molecules of both hydrogen (H_2) and oxygen (O_2) are diatomic (contain two atoms per molecule).

3. Join your oxygen and hydrogen "molecules" to form water molecules (H_2O). As you can see, two molecules of hydrogen are needed for every molecule of oxygen to form two molecules of water (Figure 10b).

What's Going On?

If a spark ignites a mixture of hydrogen and oxygen molecules, the two gases react. The atoms in the molecules rearrange, forming water molecules. The reaction is summarized by the chemical equation below:

$$2H_2 + O_2 \rightarrow 2H_2O$$

During the process a considerable amount of energy is released.

Keep Exploring—If You Have More Time!

- Use models to show how you think hydrogen (H_2) might react with chlorine (Cl_2) to form hydrogen chloride (HCl). How many hydrogen chloride molecules would be formed from one molecule of hydrogen and one molecule of chlorine?

- Under adult supervision, design and do an experiment to change water into hydrogen and oxygen. What is the volume ratio of hydrogen produced to oxygen produced?

a)

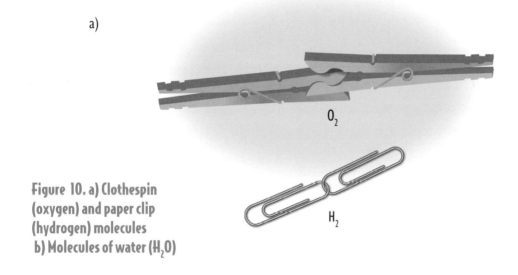

O_2

H_2

Figure 10. a) Clothespin
(oxygen) and paper clip
(hydrogen) molecules
b) Molecules of water (H_2O)

b)

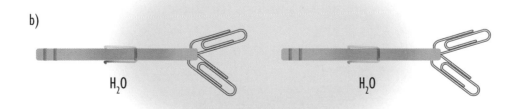

H_2O H_2O

11 Atoms Can Combine to Form Different Molecules

What's the Plan?

Let's use atomic models to see how the atoms of two elements can combine to form molecules of more than one compound.

WHAT YOU NEED:
• paper clips
• washers

What You Do

1. Gather some paper clips and washers. Let paper clips represent atoms of oxygen (O). Let washers represent atoms of carbon (C).

2. Combine an oxygen molecule (two joined paper clips) with two carbon atoms (washers) to form two molecules of carbon monoxide (CO). See Figure 11a.

3. Combine one carbon atom (a washer) with an oxygen molecule (two joined paper clips) to form one molecule of carbon dioxide (CO_2). See Figure 11b.

What's Going On?

Some elements, such as carbon and oxygen, can combine to form more than one compound. The chemical equations for these two reactions are:

$$2C + O_2 \rightarrow 2CO \qquad C + O_2 \rightarrow CO_2$$

Nitrogen and oxygen can combine to form a great many compounds—N_2O (nitrous oxide), NO (nitric oxide), N_2O_3 (dinitrogen trioxide), NO_2 (nitrogen dioxide), N_2O_4 (dinitrogen tetroxide), and N_2O_5 (dinitrogen pentoxide).

Keep Exploring—If You Have More Time!

- Use paper clips and washers as model atoms to show how nitrogen and oxygen combine to form so many compounds.

- In all the chemical equations above, use models and a balance to show that both atoms and mass are conserved.

a)

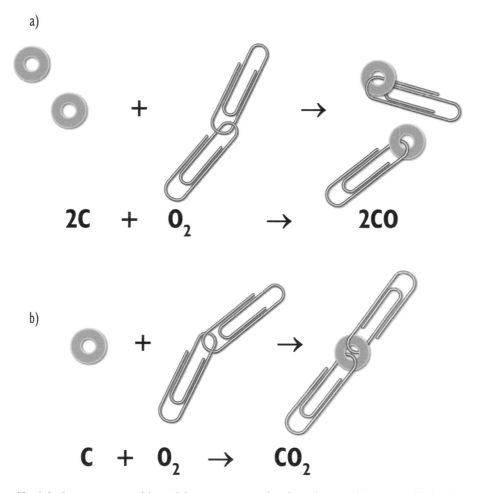

$$2C \ + \ O_2 \ \rightarrow \ 2CO$$

b)

$$C \ + \ O_2 \ \rightarrow \ CO_2$$

Figure 11. a) Carbon atoms combine with an oxygen molecule to form carbon monoxide molecules.
b) A carbon atom combines with an oxygen molecule to form a carbon dioxide molecule.

12 A Model of the States of Matter

What's the Plan?

Make a model to show how molecules exist as solid, liquid, or gas depending on temperature.

WHAT YOU NEED:

- 50 or more marbles

- a tray with steep sides or a shallow box

What You Do

1. Put fifty or more marbles in a tray (enough to cover 1/4 of the tray). Tip the tray at an angle. The marbles will collect at one end and line up in straight rows (Figure 12).

2. Keeping the tray tilted at the same angle, jiggle it gently but rapidly. Watch the marbles vibrate but remain in the same ordered arrangement.

3. Change the tilt of the tray to a smaller angle. Gradually increase the jiggling. Notice how the marbles no longer stay in ordered rows. They change positions, leaving small open spaces between them. Turn the tray. Watch the marbles "flow."

4. Put the tray on a flat surface. Shake it vigorously. The marbles now occupy the entire tray, bouncing off each other and the tray's walls in a chaotic way. The marbles "fly" in straight lines until they collide with other marbles or the tray's walls.

What's Going On?

The arrangement in step 1 represents atoms (or molecules) in solid matter. The atoms are held together in a tightly packed and orderly arrangement by attractive forces called chemical bonds.

In step 2, the model's jiggling marbles represent vibrating atoms or molecules of a solid at a higher temperature. The faster the vibrations, the higher the temperature. Notice also that the marbles take up slightly more space when they are jiggling. This explains why solids expand when heated.

In step 3, the model represents a liquid. The atoms or molecules can flow.

In step 4, the model represents a gas. The vigorous shaking, which represents high temperatures, causes vibrations so large that the atoms or molecules break completely free and become a gas.

Figure 12. A model of atoms or molecules in a solid state.

13 Atoms Are Mostly Empty

What's the Plan?

Let's try to understand why atoms are mostly empty space. The simplest atom is hydrogen. Its nucleus is a single positively charged proton. A negatively charged electron orbits the proton (Figure 13a). The nucleus's diameter is 2.4 millionths of a nanometer (nm) or 2.4 trillionths of a millimeter (mm). Scientists estimate the diameter of a hydrogen atom to be about 0.1 nm or 1/10 millionth of a millimeter. This means the diameter of a hydrogen atom is 40,000 times the diameter of its nucleus. Its radius is 20,000 times the diameter of its nucleus.

> **WHAT YOU NEED:**
> • grain of sand
> • football field or meter stick

What You Do

1. Let a grain of sand with a diameter of one millimeter (1 mm) represent the nucleus of a hydrogen atom.

2. Place the grain of sand on the goal line of a football field.

3. To gain a sense of the atom's emptiness, locate the position of the atom's electron on the football field. Remember, the distance to the electron is 20,000 times the diameter of the nucleus.

What's Going On?

There are 1,000 millimeters in a meter, so the electron will be 20 meters or 22 yards from the nucleus. Stand on the 22-yard line. Look back at the grain of sand on the goal line (Figure 13b). On the atomic scale, all that space is empty.

32

If a football field is not available, stand 20 meters (about 20 long strides) from the grain of sand.

Keep Exploring—If You Have More Time!

- People often compare an atom to the solar system. The sun represents the nucleus and the planets represent electrons orbiting the nucleus. Make a scale model of the solar system. How is it like an atom? How is it different?

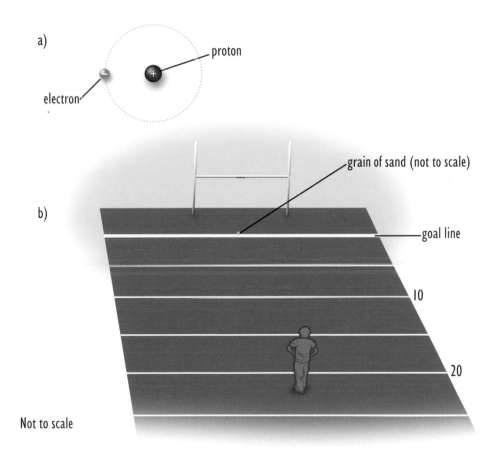

Figure 13. a) A diagram of a hydrogen atom (not to scale). b) To sense the emptiness of an atom, stand at the position of a hydrogen atom's "electron" and look back to the atom's nucleus (sand grain) 20 meters away.

5 Minutes or Less

5 min

Are you desperate? Do you have very little time to prepare a project? If so, you have come to the right place. Here are experiments you can do in about five minutes.

14 Are There Water Molecules in the Air?

What's the Plan?

Let's find out if there are water molecules in the air by doing this experiment on a warm spring or autumn day or on a rainy day in winter.

What You Do

1. Add cold water to a clear glass until it is about 2/3 full.

2. Add ice cubes until the glass is nearly full (Figure 14).

3. Wipe the outside of the glass with a towel to be sure there is no water on it.

4. Wait a few minutes. You will find water droplets collecting on the outside of the glass.

What's Going On?

Air is mostly nitrogen (78%) and oxygen (21%). However, it also contains argon (0.93%) and trace amounts of other gases, including carbon dioxide and gaseous water, which vary in amount. As Table 2 shows, the maximum amount of water that air can hold changes with temperature.

Table 2: The maximum mass of water vapor in a cubic meter of air at different temperatures.		
Air Temperature °C	°F	Maximum mass of water vapor in a cubic meter of air (grams)
0	32	4.8
10	50	9.3
20	68	17.1

When you added ice to the glass, you lowered the temperature of the air touching the glass to 0°C. If the warm air holds more than 4.8 g/m^3, water vapor will condense on the glass.

Keep Exploring—If You Have More Time!

- Someone might hypothesize that the water you found on the surface of the glass came through the glass from the inside. Design an experiment to show that such a hypothesis is not true.

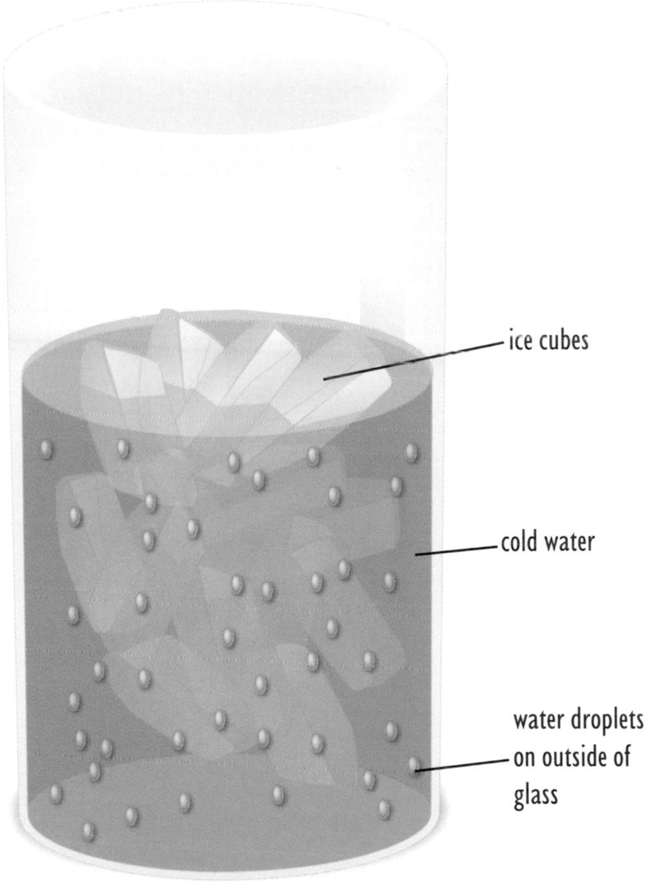

ice cubes

cold water

water droplets on outside of glass

Figure 14. Moisture (dew) collects on the outside of cold glass.

15 Even Molecules With Many Atoms Are Tiny

What's the Plan?

Let's see if we can show that even molecules with many atoms must be very small.

What You Do

1. Use an eyedropper to place one or two drops of vanilla extract inside a rubber balloon (Figure 15a).

2. Close the bottle of vanilla. Molecules of vanillin, the main ingredient in vanilla extract that have an odor, consist of 19 atoms. The chemical formula of vanillin is $C_8H_8O_3$.

3. Blow up the balloon. Then seal the neck of the balloon with a twist tie (Figure 15b).

4. Move to another room to be sure there are no vanillin molecules in the air near the balloon.

5. Move your nose around the outside of the balloon. If you can smell the vanilla, the molecules of vanillin must have come through the balloon.

What's Going On?

You could probably smell the vanilla extract when you held your nose near the balloon. That means vanillin molecules must be small enough to move between the rubber molecules in the walls of the balloon.

Keep Exploring—If You Have More Time!

- Do an experiment to see if molecules of lemon extract can pass through the walls of a balloon.

- Do an experiment to see if molecules of almond extract can pass through the walls of a balloon.

- Add vanilla extract to a balloon. Blow up the balloon and seal it. Cover the entire balloon with aluminum foil. Can you smell vanillin through the aluminum foil?

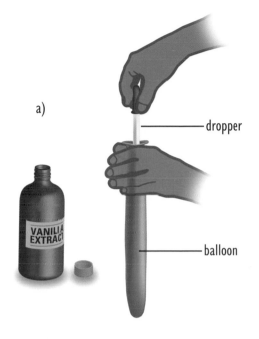

a)

dropper

balloon

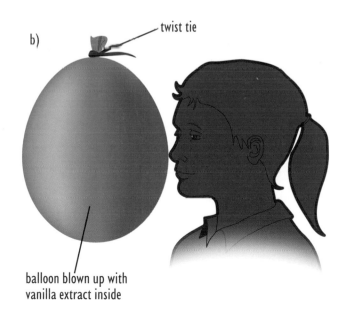

b)

twist tie

balloon blown up with vanilla extract inside

Figure 15. a) Add drops of vanilla extract to a balloon. b) Seal the balloon. Can you smell the vanillin?

37

16 Squeezing Molecules

What's the Plan?

Let's see what happens when we try to compress a gas and a liquid.

WHAT YOU NEED:

• syringe (30 mL or larger)

• water

What You Do

1. Draw some air into a syringe (Figure 16a).

2. Put a syringe cap or your finger tightly over the end of the syringe. Then try to compress the gas (Figure 16b).

3. Release the force you have applied. Watch the piston spring back to its original position.

4. Draw some water into the syringe. Put a cap or your finger tightly over the end of the syringe. Try to compress the water.

What's Going On?

Gas molecules are far apart. They occupy about a thousand times as much volume as the same number of solid or liquid molecules. Because gas molecules are far apart, they can be squeezed into a much smaller volume by applying pressure. With the molecules in a smaller volume, there will be more molecules bouncing off the walls of the container, exerting a counter pressure. When the pressure applied by your hand was released, the pressure of the enclosed air molecules caused the piston to spring back to its original position.

Liquid molecules, such as water, touch one another. There is very little space between them; consequently, liquids are practically incompressible.

Keep Exploring—If You Have More Time!

- Do an experiment to see if there is a mathematical relationship between the volume of a gas and its pressure.

- Do an experiment to find out how temperature affects the volume of a gas.

- Do an experiment to find out how temperature affects the volume of a liquid.

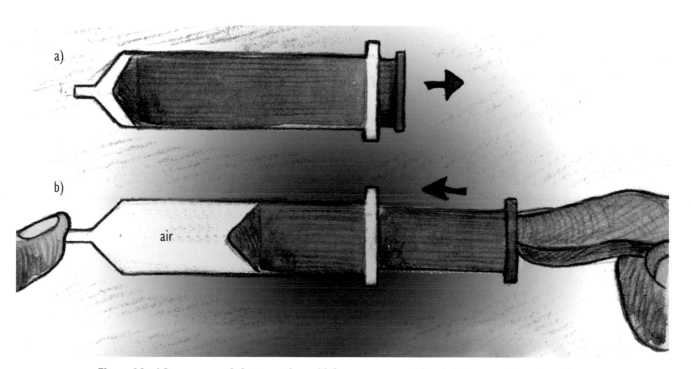

Figure 16. a) Draw some air into a syringe. b) Can you squeeze the air into a smaller volume?

17 Do Water Molecules Respond to an Electrical Charge?

WHAT YOU NEED:
- faucet
- sink
- plastic comb
- woolen cloth

What's the Plan?

Let's see if water molecules are affected by an electrical charge.

What You Do

1. Adjust a faucet so that a very thin stream of water falls into a sink.

2. Using a plastic comb, briskly comb your hair.

3. Bring the end of the comb close to the thin stream of water (Figure 17a). Watch the stream of water bend toward the comb.

4. Rub the comb with a woolen cloth.

5. Again, bring the comb near the thin stream of water. The stream will again bend toward the comb.

What's Going On?

Water molecules are polar (Figure 17b). One side of a water molecule is slightly positive; the other side is slightly negative. So either a positive or a negative charge will attract water molecules. The attraction of the water molecules for the charged comb caused the stream to bend. Electric charges accumulate on objects rubbed with a cloth or hair. In dry air, charges collect on your body when you walk on a wool rug. On a larger scale, they accumulate on clouds, causing lightning.

Keep Exploring—If You Have More Time!

- Bring a charged comb near a thin stream of cooking oil. Are cooking oil molecules polar?

- Suspend a plastic ruler from a thread. Rub the ruler with a woolen cloth. Rub a second plastic ruler with the cloth. What will happen when you bring the second ruler close to the first one? Rub a glass test tube with a silk cloth. Bring the glass near the ruler you rubbed with with wool. What happens? Are the charges on the glass the same or different from those on the ruler?

a)

b)

Figure 17. a) Bring an electrically charged comb near a thin stream of water. b) Water molecules are polar. The hydrogen end is slightly positive, and the oxygen end is slightly negative.

18 Evaporation, Temperature, and Molecular Speed

What's the Plan?

Let's see how temperature affects evaporation.

What You Do

1. Find two identical frying pans or metal pots.

2. Place a drop of water in each pan or pot.

3. Put one pan in a refrigerator.

4. Under adult supervision, place the other pan on a stove over low heat (Figure 18).

5. Watch the drop in the pan on the stove. When that drop has evaporated, look at the pan in the refrigerator. Is that drop still on the pan?

WHAT YOU NEED:

- an adult
- 2 identical frying pans or metal pots
- eyedropper
- water
- stove
- refrigerator

What's Going On?

You probably found that the drop in the pan on the stove evaporated faster than the drop in the refrigerator. Adding heat to molecules gives them more kinetic (motion) energy. They move faster, on the average, than molecules at a lower temperature. It is the faster moving molecules in a liquid that can escape from the liquid and become a gas. By adding heat to the water in the pan on the stove, you gave those water molecules more energy than the cooler molecules in the refrigerator. As a result, the warmer, faster moving molecules changed to a gas before the cooler, slower moving ones.

Keep Exploring—If You Have More Time!

- Design and carry out an experiment to show how surface area affects the rate at which water evaporates.

- Design and carry out an experiment to show how wind affects the rate at which water evaporates.

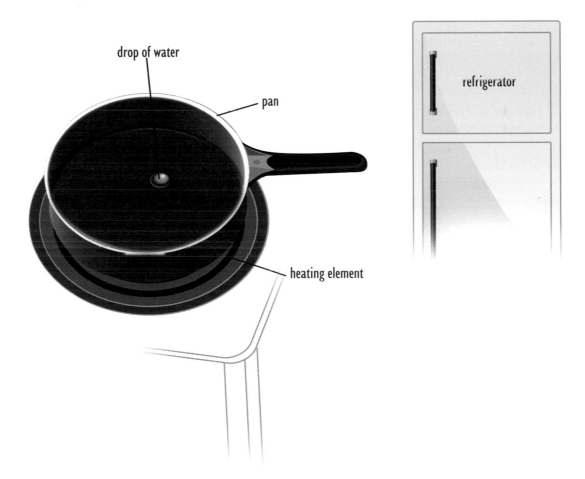

Figure 18. Which water drop will evaporate faster? The one in the pan or the one in the refrigerator?

Words to Know

atom—The smallest particle that makes up an element. All atoms of the same element have the same number of protons in a tiny nucleus and an equal number of electrons that orbit the nucleus. Atoms are smaller than a nanometer.

atomic nuclei—The positively charged centers of atoms. The nuclei usually consist of tightly packed positively charged protons and uncharged neutrons. Most hydrogen nuclei consist of a single proton and no neutrons. These nuclei are extremely small, on the order of trillionths of a millimeter.

carbon dioxide (CO_2)—A gas, more dense than air, with a molecular mass of 44 AMU that does not support combustion and, therefore, is used in some fire extinguishers.

cubic close packing—The way the ions of sodium chloride and other compounds are arranged in a crystal.

elastic collision—A collision in which no kinetic (motion) energy is lost. Most atomic and molecular collisions are elastic.

electrons—Negatively charged particles found outside the nuclei of atoms. The electrons orbit the positively charged nuclei of atoms.

evaporation—The change of a substance from the liquid to the gaseous state.

gas—A state of matter in which the atoms or molecules are far apart. As a result, a gas can be compressed to a much smaller volume.

gas thermometer—A device that measures temperature by the amount of expansion or contraction of a gas.

inelastic collision—A collision in which all the kinetic (motion) energy disappears. The kinetic energy is converted to thermal (heat) energy.

ions—Atoms that have lost or gained an electron. Since electrons carry one negative charge, atoms that lose an electron have a positive charge. Atoms that gain an electron have a negative charge.

model—An object used to represent something else. For example, you might use a washer to represent an atom of a particular element.

molecule—The smallest particle of an element or compound that has the properties of the element or compound. The molecule is made up of one or more atoms bonded together in a fixed whole number ratio.

nanometer (nm)—A billionth of a meter.

pi (π)—The ratio of the circumference of a circle to its diameter (C/d), which is approximately 3.14.

polar molecules—The electrical charges in polar molecules are not distributed evenly. As a result, one part of the molecule has a slight positive charge, and another part will have a slight negative charge.

states of matter—Matter can exist in three states—solid, liquid, or gas.

temperature—A measure of the average speed of atoms or molecules.

Further Reading

Books

Aloian, Molly. *Atoms and Molecules.* New York: Crabtree Publishing Company, 2009.

Bardhan-Quallen, Sudipta. *Championship Science Fair Projects: 100 Sure-to-Win Experiments.* New York: Scholastic, 2005.

Bochinski, Julianne Blair. *More Award-Winning Science Fair Projects.* Hoboken, N.J.: John Wiley and Sons, 2004.

Cregan, Elizabeth R. C. *The Atom.* Mankato, Minn.: Compass Point Books, 2009.

DiSpezio, Michael A. *Super Sensational Science Fair Projects.* New York: Sterling Publishers, 2004.

Fox, Karen C. *Older Than the Stars.* Watertown, Mass.: Charlesbridge Publishing, 2011.

Friedhoffer, Bob. *Everything You Need for Winning Science Fair Projects.* New York: Chelsea House, 2006.

Juettner, Bonnie. *Molecules.* Farmington Hills, Mich.: Kidhaven Press, 2005.

Rhatigan, Joe, and Rain Newcomb. *Prize-Winning Science Fair Projects for Curious Kids.* New York: Lark Books, 2006.

Internet Addresses

Science Kids at Home: How Do Atoms Bond?
<http://www.sciencekidsathome.com/science_topics/how_do_atoms_bond.html>

Science Kids: Chemistry Videos
<http://www.sciencekids.co.nz/videos/chemistry.html>

Index